ARTIST TRANSCRIPTIONS

Transcribed by Dan Rodowicz

KENNY G TH

MW00564320

CONTENTS

Cover Photo: Matthew Rolston

ISBN 978-0-7935-7396-7

7777 W. BLUEMOUND RD. P.O. BOX 13819 MILWAUKEE, WI 53213

Visit Hal Leonard Online at
www.halleonard.com

The Moment

By Kenny G

Slowly, tenderly (♩ = 91)

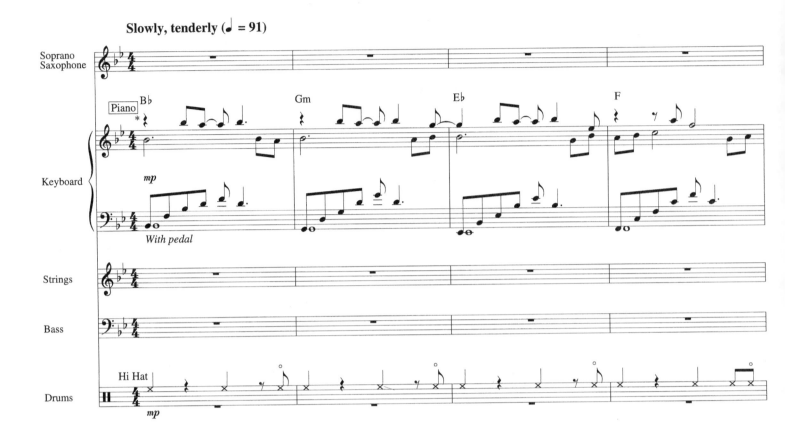

* Piano part is played on 2 tracks

4

6

Passages

By Kenny G

12

14

Havana

By Kenny G and Walter Afanasieff

Slowly, somewhat freely

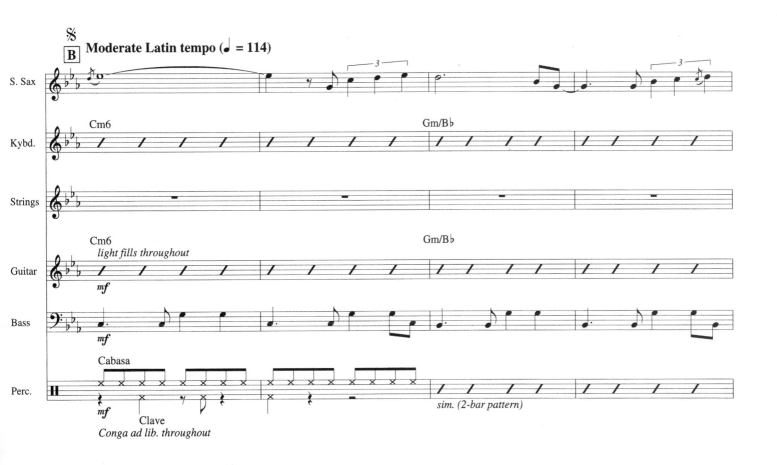

18

Always

By Kenny G

24

26

That Somebody Was You

Words and Music by Kenny G, Walter Afanasieff and Babyface

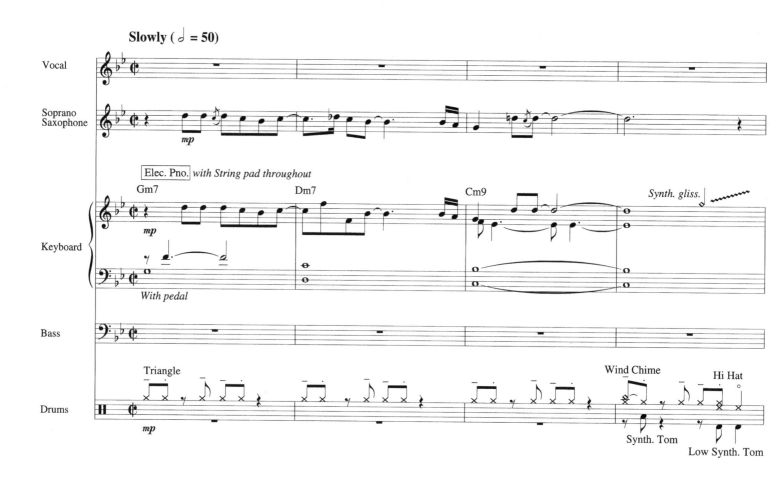

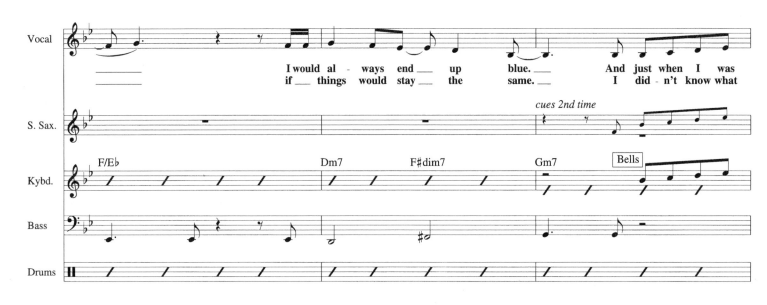

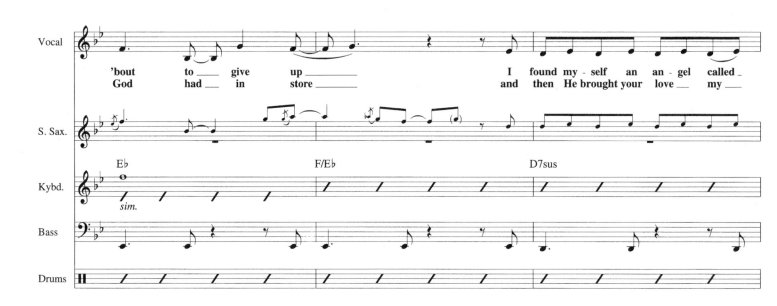

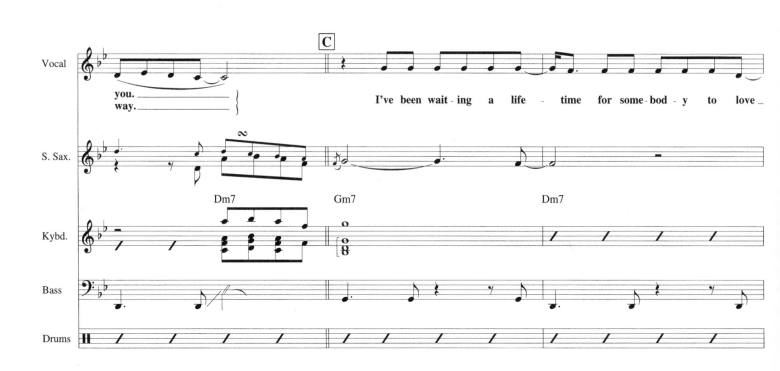

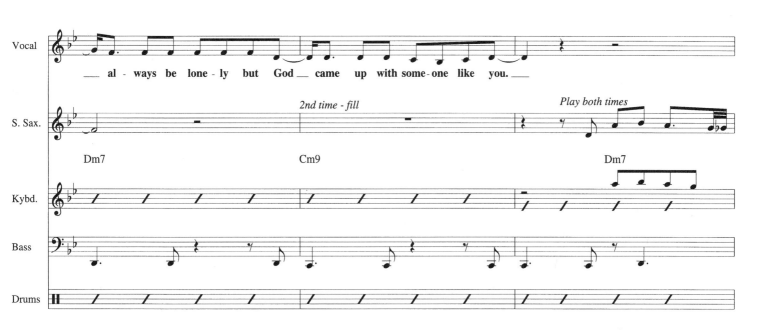

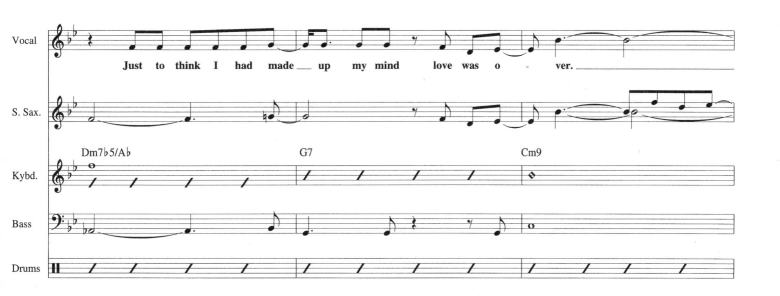

32

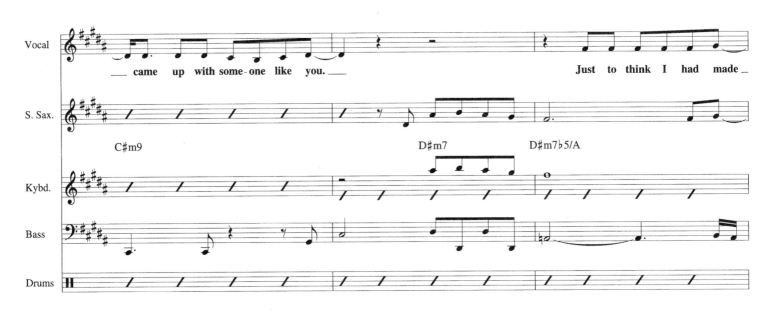

The Champion's Theme

By Kenny G and Walter Afanasieff

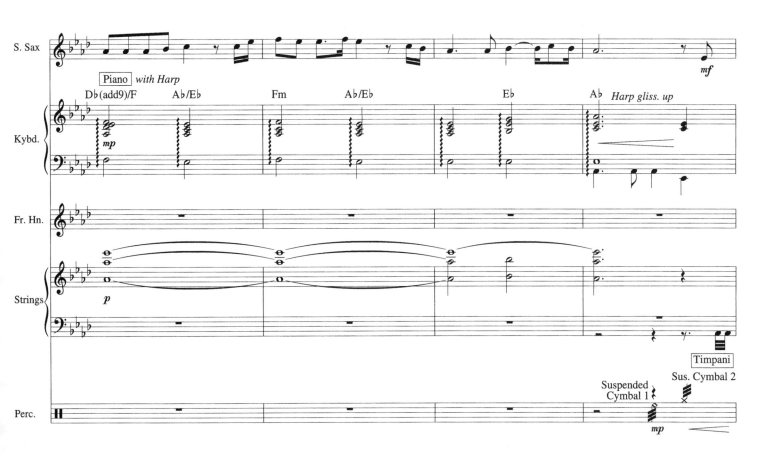

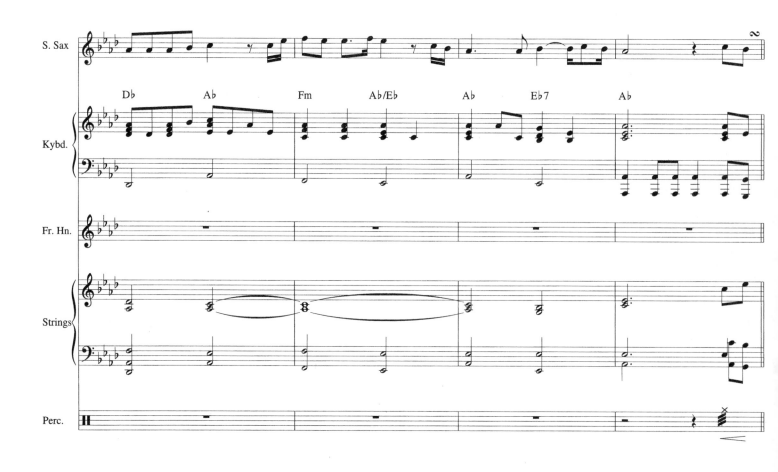

42

Eastside Jam

By Kenny G

* Same octave as it sounds

sim. (4 bar pattern)

(Solo ends)

Moonlight

By Kenny G and Walter Afanasieff

58

Gettin' on the Step

By Kenny G and Walter Afanasieff

62

Everytime I Close My Eyes

Words and Music by Babyface

64

2nd time-Snare Drum (not cross stick)

Northern Lights

By Kenny G and Walter Afanasieff

74

Innocence

By Kenny G and Walter Afanasieff

78

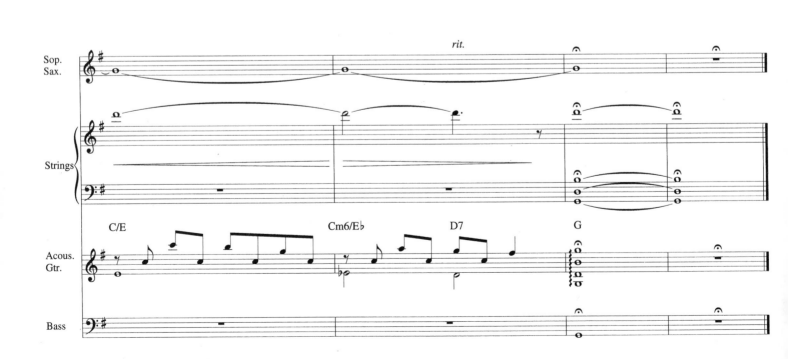